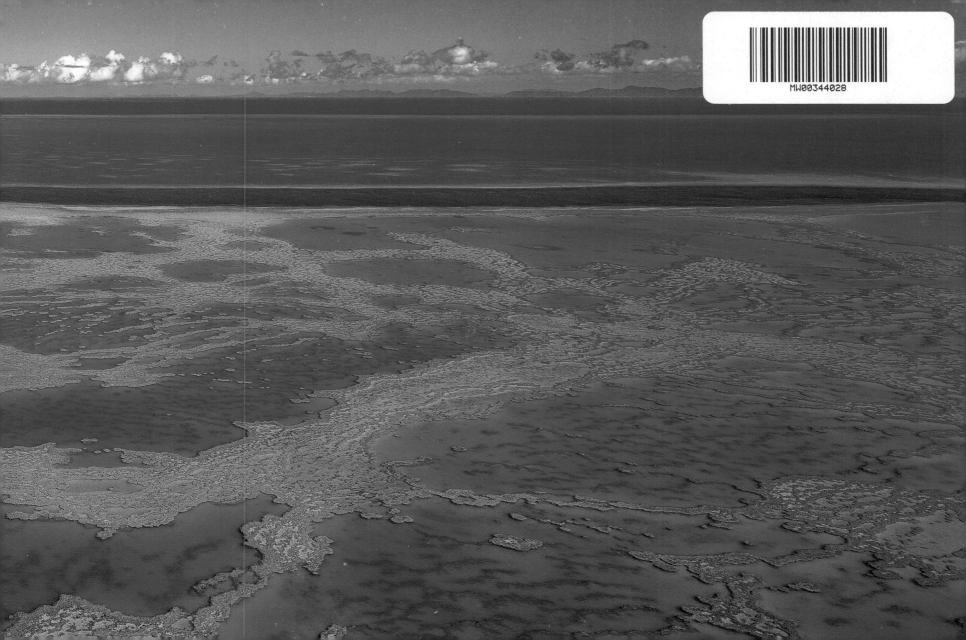

AUSTRALIA WIDE

A sensational panoramic journey

PANOGRAPHS®
PUBLISHING PTY LTD

Australia's treasure lies in its superb natural heritage. In the red-dust deserts of the Outback, or along the beaches of Australia's sun-soaked north, we draw close to the living heart of a remarkable land.

Australia is frontier country, where people may still walk freely amid pristine wilderness, feeling its power and majesty. Under the rainforest canopies and the immense desert sky, beside still pools and flowing waterfalls, the natural world casts its illuminating light upon our own lives.

When we reflect on the beauty of God's creation, we are better able to put things in perspective. Our own lives are truly small compared with the vast world around us. We are linked with the beauty of nature. If we take the time to enjoy it, it will nourish our souls.

Ken Duncan

TITLE PAGE
Palm Cove, Cairns, Qld

LEFT
Russell Falls, Tas

Ken Duncan (OAM) was born in Mildura, Victoria, in 1954. A professional photographer since 1980, his work has received many industry awards both in Australia and overseas, and he is now recognized as one of the world's leading panoramic landscape specialists.

Typically casual about such accolades, Ken prefers to say he is just an average photographer with a mighty God. His goal and passion in life is simply to show people the beauty of God's creation, encouraging them to look beyond themselves to something far greater.

Enjoy the journey as you wander with Ken through the pages of this book, experiencing the wonder of Australia's natural heritage.

RIGHT
Sunset, Bunyeroo Creek, Flinders Ranges, SA

A classic tropical island – topped with a red-roofed lighthouse – luxuriates in the blue. Here it is not only the island that beckons, but also the sea. The turquoise of the water is wonderfully textured by the coral reef below, like an open invitation to explore its submerged treasures. This shot was taken in the wet season. In the distance can be seen the brooding "cloud mountains" of a tropical storm, darkening the rainforests of the coast. Few people visit Australia's north during the wet. Yet this photograph reminds us that every season has its own distinct glory. We are richer when we enjoy beauty in all its forms.

PREVIOUS PAGES
Atlantis Falls, Kimberley, WA

LEFT
Lowe Isles, Qld

This mid-morning shot captures Cape Peron in a deep red blaze of glory. Although the Cape is actually part of the mainland, from this angle it has all the appearance of a desert island in the midst of the ocean. The colours are thrown boldly into the sea as the waves lap gently at the contrasting swathe of pure white sand. I set my Roundshot camera low over the waves to capture this shot. A two-foot wave rolling in from behind would have trashed my gear! But thankfully the sea remained calm for just long enough, and I was able to record this very unusual view.

RIGHT
Desert island, WA

OVERLEAF
Sunrise, Norah Head Lighthouse, NSW

ABOVE
Hill Inlet, Qld

Located not far from the main expressway to Sydney, Somersby Falls is one of the most picturesque locations on the NSW Central Coast. The odd thing is that so few locals go there. They have seen the signs, but have never taken the turn off; and many of those who do visit only visit the Falls once – just so they can tick it off their list. Yet places like this deserve many revisitings. Different seasons and weather conditions reveal entirely new moods, and there are always new details to be noticed among the melaleuca trees and moss-covered rocks. In fact, this cascade is only the top-most (and most accessible) of a whole series of falls. For those who take the time to explore further downstream, there are even more delights to discover.

RIGHT
Somersby sanctuary, NSW

An afterglow of rich late-afternoon light plays beautifully upon the mineralised rock strata of Hamersley Gorge. The haunting majesty of the scene is strengthened by the dramatic folds of the land, and by the stillness of the spring-fed waters as they reflect the silent trees. Located in Western Australia's Pilbara region (famous for its vast mineral deposits and mining), Hamersley Gorge provides a rare escape from the surrounding harshness, and from the fierce heat, which can top fifty degrees Celsius. It is a hidden oasis amid a land of inhospitable rock and Spinifex, more than welcome as a refuge for travellers who pass this way.

LEFT
Hamersley Gorge, WA

OVERLEAF
Raining on the rock, Uluru, NT

We were the first summer group of 2008 to reach these famous huts, located in one of the most hostile regions of Antarctica. We had to wait until the winds subsided to make landfall, then dig out the snow to access the buildings. This was the tiny base camp of the famous Australasian Antarctic Expedition, led by Douglas Mawson in 1911–1914. I shot this photograph when just a little bit of light miraculously penetrated the clouds. Inside the huts I saw where renowned photographer Frank Hurley had his dark room (there were still chemicals there). More essential restoration still needs to be done on these iconic structures, yet work will always be difficult here. Even as we left, the ice floes closed in. It took one and a half days – with many concerned looks from the crew – to get our cruise ship clear again and away.

RIGHT
Mawson's Huts, Antarctica

Who would think it possible? Deep in the Great Southern Ocean, on the cold, misty desolation that is Macquarie Island, a large colony of penguins not only survives but thrives. Although this shot was taken in summer, the day was wild and bitterly cold. We had a lengthy wait for just a bit of sunlight to break through and illuminate this scene. Most of the penguins here are Royal Penguins, though one or two of the larger King Penguins can also be seen. In the mid-ground, on the right, is a sprawling group of huge elephant seals. The waters here must be teeming with food to support such a vast assembly of creatures. How wonderful is the abundance of life in our world!

LEFT
Royal gathering, Macquarie Island

ABOVE
Nature's fishermen, Terrigal, NSW

ABOVE
Penguin promenade, Macquarie Island

Patience is a great virtue in life and can often be one of the hardest to achieve. Landscape photography has been very good for me in this respect. To get this shot I had to turn up faithfully day after day for weeks, waiting for the right light. It is helpful to realise that we are not always in control of our circumstances, only our attitudes to them. So often we can miss our miracles because we get discouraged and give up just before the breakthrough comes.

PREVIOUS PAGES
Ormiston Gorge, West MacDonnell Ranges, NT

RIGHT
Faithful guardians, The Twelve Apostles, Vic

LEFT
The Spout,
Liffey Falls State Reserve, Tas

OVERLEAF
King George Falls, Kimberley, WA

ABOVE
River song, Hopetoun Falls, Vic

Having somewhat messed up our directions, we arrived at this location (Cathedral Rocks, near Kiama) later in the afternoon than we intended. The rainbow appeared just as we arrived. There was a sudden scramble of activity as I attempted to capture this wonderfully magnificent but fleeting moment. I didn't even have time to take proper light readings, and only managed two exposures before both the light and the rainbow disappeared. In spite of all this, the shot worked beautifully. I was so grateful. It was a wonderful gift from the Creator – an emotive drama of sea and sky signed off with the promise of a rainbow.

LEFT
Cathedral Rocks, near Kiama, NSW

RIGHT
Cape Wickham Lighthouse,
King Island, Tas

OVERLEAF
Sunset, Anson Bay, Norfolk Island

Incredible textures mix and merge in this dramatic wet season panorama off the Kimberley coast. We had reached this reef by boat then taken off in a helicopter for an aerial view. But we only had moments for a couple of shots (this was one of them) before the mountainous, fast-approaching storm forced our quick retreat. The pilot showed incredible skill to land the helicopter on the already pitching boat before the tempest engulfed us with its huge drops and unbelievable amounts of rain. But we got away safely, and we had this spectacular photograph to commemorate our day. Often in life, it is the stormy seasons that yield the greatest glories.

LEFT
Montgomery Reef, WA

Autumn brings a spray of vibrant colour to a garden in the Blue Mountains. It is like a meeting of the hemispheres, a touch of New England amid the old native gums. The light is soft and dappled, with many nooks slipping away into shadow. A leaf-strewn path draws the viewer deep into the glade. Behind it all, the sky appears like a whitewash, far removed from the vivid blue of summer and yet accentuating the colours of the fading leaves. Scenes such as this serve to remind us of the steady march of the seasons. The bright hues of autumn herald the approach of winter, yet warmth and new life will soon return with the spring. In nature everything has its cycle. Nothing is static. All of creation is renewed each year.

RIGHT
Autumn, Mount Wilson, NSW

ABOVE
Kimberley boabs, WA

ABOVE
God's Marbles, Wauchope, NT

PREVIOUS PAGES
Moroka Hut,
Alpine National Park, Vic

RIGHT
Sunrise, Wamberal Beach, NSW

Early morning near Eudunda in South Australia reveals an old stone hut in a sea of green. The sky is a blur of pastel, the hills crowned with a delicate mist. Seen here just after rain, this is the sort of view that must have greeted the old pioneers in the good years. In times of drought these fields would have turned to straw, but with the rains would have come a certain bounty. We can almost imagine a farmer at work in the distance, with his young wife and children busy perhaps in the yard. Those days are long gone but the heritage of those years survives. The fields have been tamed; the stone cottage may well endure for centuries. Our nation has been built in large measure by our pioneers. We do well when we remember their legacy.

LEFT
Pioneer cottage, SA

This image was taken at Picnic Rocks on Tasmania's east coast. The sunset had been golden, crowned in glory and majesty; I had been about to leave, thinking surely it couldn't get any better. But I decided to stay on, and as I did the sunset evolved into this beautiful lingering pastel vision. Everything was so subtle and soft and there was a pervading calm. Then the curtain was slowly drawn on the day as the sky went from a beautiful pink to a powdery blue to a midnight blue – until the day was gone. Scenery like this helps put into perspective the problems that often confront us. When we witness the beauty of such magical moments, there is an overwhelming sense of peace.

RIGHT
Afterglow, Tas

ABOVE
Mossman Gorge, Mossman, Qld

ABOVE
Sunrise, The Nut, Stanley, Tas

Shadows creep into the valleys and ravines of Kata Tjuta as night approaches and the land prepares for the hush of darkness. Like Uluru situated thirty kilometres to the east, this extensive maze of domes is an ancient focus of Aboriginal life and beliefs. To stand within its towering amphitheater is to feel close to the heart of creation. Here, the late afternoon sun shoots beneath the clouds and illuminates its rich red tones.

LEFT
Sunset, Kata Tjuta, NT

RIGHT
The Remarkables,
Kangaroo Island, SA

ABOVE
Peaceful waters, Coles Bay, Tas

ABOVE
Murray River jetty, SA

PREVIOUS PAGES
Tulips, Wynyard, Tas

RIGHT
Kakadu Dreaming, NT

It took a massive drive – crossing some serious rivers on the long Cape York Track – to reach this little piece of paradise. But what a sanctuary we discovered it to be. Here Chilli Beach lay dreamily in the tropical sun. The brilliant blues of sky and water merged, and the sand – pristine and white – stretched lazily into the distance. To pass the time while waiting for the right light, we invented a new leisure activity: playing coconut bowls with all the scattered nuts from the palms! I call this shot "Imagine", because I love the idea of just dreaming I am here even when back among the stresses of normal workaday life. It's a scene to get lost in. Just listen for the surf lapping the sand and for the breeze coursing through the palm fronds. Here, where there are no footprints, imagine making your own.

LEFT
Imagine, Chilli Beach, Qld

ABOVE
Silverton, NSW

AUSTRALIA WIDE
First published 2010
by Panographs Publishing Pty Ltd
ABN 21 050 235 606
PO Box 3015, Wamberal, NSW, 2260, Australia
Telephone +61 2 4367 6777
Email: panos@kenduncan.com

Panographs is a registered trademark
of the Ken Duncan Group Pty Limited.
Photography and text by Ken Duncan
©2010 Divine Guidance P/L
Designed by Good Catch Design
Edited by Peter Friend
Reprographics by CFL Print Studio
Printed and bound in China

National Library of Australia Cataloguing-in-
Publication entry
Author: Duncan, Ken.
Title: Australia wide : a sensational panoramic
journey / author and photographer Ken Duncan.
ISBN: 9780980527827 (hbk.)
Subjects: Landscape photography-Australia.
Australia-Pictorial works.
Dewey Number: 919.400222

- **414 The Entrance Road, Erina Heights, NSW**
  Telephone +61 2 4367 6701
- **73 George Street, The Rocks, Sydney, NSW**
  Telephone +61 2 9241 3460
- **Level 1, 9 Star Circus, Harbour Town**
  Shopping Centre, Docklands, Vic
  Telephone +61 3 9670 6971
- **Shop 14 Hunter Valley Gardens Village,**
  Broke Road, Pokolbin, NSW
  Telephone +61 2 4998 6711
- **63 Abbott Street, Cairns, Qld**
  Telephone +61 7 4051 3999